SCULPTED
THREADS

Artful Brooches, Earrings,
and More

JANET SHIPLEY HAWKS

Martingale®
& C O M P A N Y

Sculpted Threads
Artful Brooches, Earrings, and More
© 2007 by Janet Shipley Hawks

That Patchwork Place® is an imprint of Martingale & Company®.

Martingale & Company
20205 144th Ave. NE
Woodinville, WA 98072-8478
www.martingale-pub.com

Printed in China
12 11 10 09 08 07   8 7 6 5 4 3 2 1

Library of Congress Cataloging-in-Publication Data
Library of Congress Control Number: 2007007218

ISBN: 978-1-56477-728-7

CREDITS

President & CEO • Tom Wierzbicki

Publisher • Jane Hamada

Editorial Director • Mary V. Green

Managing Editor • Tina Cook

Technical Editor • Dawn Anderson

Copy Editor • Melissa Bryan

Design Director • Stan Green

Illustrator • Robin Strobel

Cover & Text Designer • Shelly Garrison

Photographer • Brent Kane

MISSION STATEMENT
Dedicated to providing quality products
and service to inspire creativity.

DEDICATION

To the memory of the women who introduced me to the sewing machine and taught me how to use it: my grandmother, my mother, my aunt, and my home economics teacher. I'm sure they'd be surprised at how I use one now, and I hope they would be pleased.

ACKNOWLEDGMENTS

Thanks to Amy Stewart Winsor, who suggested the idea of a book and then insisted that I pursue it.

Thanks to the family that taught me patience and perseverance, those who taught me the skills, and all who have encouraged me in all my artistic endeavors.

A very special thanks to my husband, Bob, who encouraged, supported, and helped me in so many ways throughout the process. Without him it wouldn't have happened.

Contents

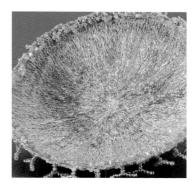

Introduction

The sculpted-threads technique has evolved as a result of one of those "Why couldn't I...?" moments that came when I was envisioning a special Christmas gift for friends who were both artists. Many years before, I had heard a woman in a very small gallery explain that she had an art piece made of thread. At the time I didn't pursue what kind of thread or how it was done; it just seemed to go in one ear and out the other. But something did remain. I began to experiment with water-soluble stabilizer and the beautiful colors of machine-embroidery thread, and the fiber-art form I call "sculpted threads" was born. My first creations were bowls, as I was somewhat influenced by the work of my husband, who is a wood turner. The Christmas gift was a success and I was so encouraged by its reception that I continued to experiment and develop other items made with thread. I've sewed miles of thread onto yards of stabilizer and enjoyed it all. I hope my experience will encourage you to try your hand at creating something all your own, even if you've never created an original piece of art.

Sculpted-Threads Basics

Beautiful thread vessels, jewelry, and accessories can be created by free-motion stitching with machine-embroidery thread onto water-soluble stabilizer. Stitching is done in layers, or rounds, to produce flat as well as shaped forms. When the project is completed, the stabilizer is removed by immersing the work in water, leaving only the thread, which supports itself. The sculpted-threads piece is then shaped and allowed to dry. The basic techniques will be discussed in this section, and then referred to again in future sections.

The sculpted-threads technique is fun for making creative, original works—not projects with scientific accuracy. There is no right or wrong way to make these pieces, although some techniques work better than others. If a certain color doesn't seem right, it's usually possible to stitch over it or embellish heavily in that area to change the appearance. So relax and enjoy the colors and the creative process.

Sewing-Machine Basics

All the sculpted-threads projects in this book involve the use of free-motion stitching. There are just a few things to be aware of when setting up your machine to create with thread.

MACHINE REQUIREMENTS

Since these projects are made using free-motion machine stitching, it's necessary to drop the feed dogs on your sewing machine, but it's not necessary to have the latest computer-driven, top-of-the-line machine for these projects. If dropping the feed dogs is a procedure that is unfamiliar to you, check your sewing machine's manual for instructions on performing this task. Sculpted-threads projects require many more stitches than normal sewing or even free-motion quilting, so be sure to keep the machine cleaned and maintained as recommended by the manufacturer. Try not to get frustrated with broken needles and threads, as they can both be fixed.

TENSION

Even though you'll be doing free-motion stitching on these projects, it's important for your stitches to be balanced. Sometimes the project is made with different colors or types of thread in the bobbin and the needle, and it's not desirable to have the contrasting thread showing on the opposite side of the work. To test for balance, before dropping the feed dogs, stitch a regular straight stitch with different colors of machine-embroidery thread in the bobbin and the needle, and then adjust the tension according to the manufacturer's directions.

FREE-MOTION FEET

A free-motion or darning foot allows the project to move freely under the presser foot while you are free-motion stitching. The free-motion foot must be in the down position to form stitches. If it isn't down, there is no tension on the top thread and the result will be a large tangle of thread around the bobbin.

Many machines come with free-motion, or darning, feet, or you may purchase these feet as an accessory (see "Resources" on page 63). Some machines have a "darning" position on the presser foot lifter, which results in a space between the foot and the bed of the machine so the work may be moved freely. Check your machine's instruction manual under "darning" for explanations of these features.

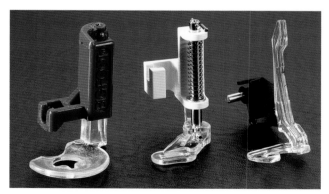

Free-motion feet, often referred to as darning feet, may be generic or manufacturer specific.

SEWING-MACHINE NEEDLES

For these projects, you'll achieve the best results by using fairly large sewing-machine needles. Because the work gets thicker as more layers of stitching are applied, a size 14 (90) or 16 (100) jeans or topstitching needle will penetrate much better than a smaller needle. When stitching a vessel, I advise using a size 16 (100) or 18 (110) jeans or topstitching needle, as the layers are even thicker and harder to penetrate. Needles made specifically for metallic threads are a must, in at least a size 14 (90), if using metallic thread on the top of your project. Be sure that the needle is properly seated and securely fastened before starting to stitch. After you insert and tighten a needle, gently lower and raise it by hand to check the alignment before threading and starting to stitch.

The needles should be designated as topstitching, jeans, or universal type, but not ball point. Needles can break during free-motion stitching, so I recommend wearing eye protection and keeping extra needles on hand. Some mail-order and Internet sources have needles available in bulk, and some offer specials when you buy several packages (see "Resources" on page 63).

Basic Supplies

The sculpted-threads projects are created with very few supplies, the main ones being thread and stabilizer. To create jewelry or decorative bags, you'll also need a few finishing supplies, and you may want to embellish vessels or jewelry with some simple beading.

THREAD AND THREAD ACCESSORIES

Thread manufacturers are designing many products for machine embroidery today as a result of the great popularity of home-embroidery machines. You can find embroidery threads made of rayon, acrylic, polyester, holographic, and metallic materials, and they're available in wonderfully vibrant colors and variegations. Threads made specifically for machine quilting are generally cotton and don't have the luster of machine-embroidery threads, but they're available in variegated colors and are acceptable for sculpted-threads projects. Metallic

threads are delicate and more difficult to work with; I find they're less prone to breakage in the bobbin than in the needle.

Vibrant colors abound in machine-embroidery threads.

Some threads come on cones, while others are available on various sizes and styles of spools. A freestanding cone holder is a helpful piece of equipment for cones of thread. It saves frustration by allowing the thread to feed smoothly. Cone holders are available in notions departments and by mail order (see "Resources" on page 63).

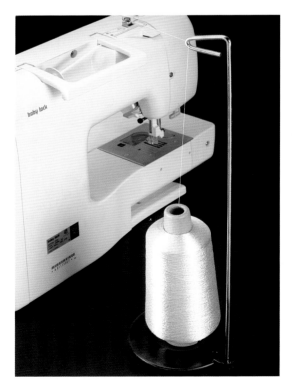

A cone holder is a useful accessory.

Another handy accessory is a spool holder that slips onto your sewing machine's built-in holder and changes the position of a spool from vertical to horizontal and vice versa (see "Resources" on page 63). This allows a spool to turn rather than the thread being pulled off over the end of the spool. This is especially important if using flat threads such as the metallic and holographic types in the needle, and it's also important when winding bobbins. If the thread is pulled over the end of the spool, it twists, causing breakage and certain frustration.

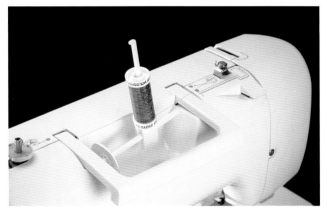

A spool holder allows the spool to turn.

Large areas of one flat color are not as interesting as variations in shade of one color or the combination of two colors. By using different threads in the needle and the bobbin and turning the stabilizer over after stitching a layer, it's possible to mix two threads or colors and add depth and interest to any piece. Metallic thread is best saved for the middle or top layers, where it will be more visible than in the initial layers. Remember to use the metallic thread in the bobbin, as it breaks more easily when it's threaded in the needle.

STABILIZER

There are many stabilizers available through stores, catalogs, and online as a result of the influx of home-embroidery machines. Sculpted-threads projects are done on water-soluble stabilizer. The most common form of this has the appearance of clear vinyl and comes in light, medium, and heavy weights. The heavyweight stabilizer is what I recommend for these projects. The shape to be stitched can be marked on the stabilizer using a grease pencil or a felt-tip marker.

If heavyweight stabilizer isn't available, the mediumweight type may be used for small projects by layering at least two thicknesses and treating them as one. If using mediumweight stabilizer, be sure to place the layers in a hoop when starting the project to help prevent the puckering and tearing that can result from stitches cutting through the stabilizer.

Recently, a nonwoven water-soluble stabilizer has become available. It's a white, opaque material that feels like fabric but dissolves in water. None of the projects in this book have been tested using this new stabilizer.

Water-soluble stabilizers come in several weights. The heaviest is recommended for sculpted-threads projects.

There is also a water-soluble stabilizer that has a sticky side for adhering to the wrong side of fabric when doing machine embroidery. This *will not work* for sculpted-threads projects, so be sure to read the package labeling carefully.

Water-soluble stabilizer is a flexible material that will stretch and pucker as stitches are added. The form pulls in somewhat, which is particularly noticeable when creating small elements for jewelry pieces, so you must take that into consideration when laying out the initial shape and size of your pieces. In some applications stretching is desirable, while in others it's to be prevented to keep the work flat.

If the stabilizer is left out in the open, it becomes less pliable and, though it will still support the stitches, it will be more difficult to use. Be sure to keep the unused portion of the stabilizer in a closed plastic bag to preserve the flexibility of the product. It's also a good idea, particularly in dry conditions, to place works in progress in a plastic bag between sewing sessions.

For some projects, the stabilizer may not be wide enough or, when starting a vessel, you might not be able to visualize the finished size. It's quite easy to put two pieces of stabilizer together before starting the project or to add another piece of stabilizer to the edges of the starting piece to gain extra space for doing the work. A larger work surface can also help to protect fingers from the needle while stitching. To add a piece of stabilizer, dampen the edge of one piece slightly and overlap it with another piece by ¼" or less. You need only a slight bit of water to make the pieces stick together—too much moisture can make them soft and sticky. Be sure to let the stabilizer dry completely. Pieces of stabilizer can also be stitched together if dampening isn't convenient.

HOOPS

Embroidery hoops are helpful when starting out if using lightweight or mediumweight stabilizer or when working with small pieces such as earrings. The easiest hoops to use are the thin plastic ones with a metal spring that secures the stabilizer. They come in many sizes and should be at least 2" larger than your design so that the retaining screw on the needle assembly does not hit the finger loops on the hoop during stitching.

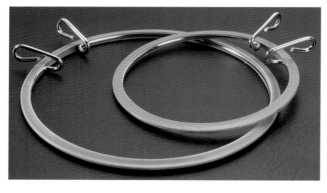

Thin hoops are easy to slip under the free-motion foot on the sewing machine.

Stitching Basics

All the sculpted-threads projects are composed of zigzag stitches, straight stitches, or a combination of both. Using different stitches at different stages and in a varying manner helps form the shapes. I recommend setting the stitch length at zero so the dropped feed dogs won't move. Stitch length is determined by the speed of the machine and how quickly or slowly the stabilizer is moved. Generally, the faster you run the machine, the faster you need to move the work under the needle.

STITCHING FLAT FORMS

Flat forms such as those used in geometric brooches on pages 16–21 are stitched with closely spaced rows of stitching in layers. Each layer of thread is stitched at a 90° angle from the previous layer. It is best to move the stabilizer in a front-to-back motion when stitching. This allows for better precision and creates a piece that resembles woven fabric. It's also acceptable to work side to side, but control on smaller pieces, such as earrings, seems better with front-to-back stitching.

STITCHING CIRCULAR FORMS

Circular forms with "stretched edges" are stitched in a pattern radiating from the center to the outer edge. The base for these pieces is a wheel of spokes created by repeatedly dividing the circle. This method creates an evenly distributed base for the rest of the stitching. To stitch circular forms:

1. Draw a circle on the stabilizer and then draw perpendicular lines through the center. Mark the end of one of these lines with an arrow outside the circle to indicate your starting line, and write "side one" in the upper-left corner of the stabilizer.

2. Starting at the center, zigzag stitch along the starting line to the outer edge of the circle. Stop and then retrace the stitching back through the center and continue to the opposite side. Stop on the outer edge of the circle and retrace the

stitching back to the center. Pivot the stabilizer 90° and stitch from the center to the outer edge, back through the center, to the opposite edge, and back to the center. There are now four spokes in the circle.

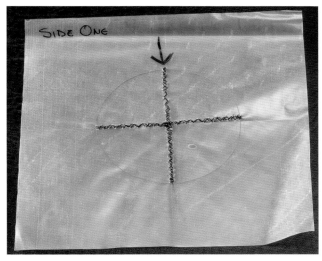

On heavyweight stabilizer, stitch four spokes within the circle.

3. Continue stitching in this manner and bisecting the spaces created until there are 16 spokes.

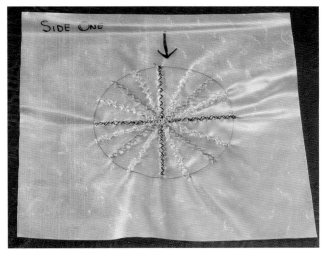

There are now 16 spokes. For clarity, the first 4 were stitched in black, the next 4 in red, and the remaining 8 in turquoise.

4. From this point on, continue adding "spokes" between each row of stitching, but don't pass

over the center as it will become too thick if all spokes cross that point.

A circular piece becomes dense in the center after 128 spokes have been stitched.

The instructions for each circular piece shown in the book will indicate the number of spokes that should be stitched for each layer. On the larger circles, some layers of stitching will be done only on the outside edge of the circle to help keep the thickness of the piece more even. The instructions will indicate how far in from the edge to stitch. If no indication is made, the stitching is done from the edge toward the center. Reverse the stitching and return to the edge when the thickest part is reached at the center. For a more delicate, feathered appearance, vary the length of the ends of the stitching at the outside edge.

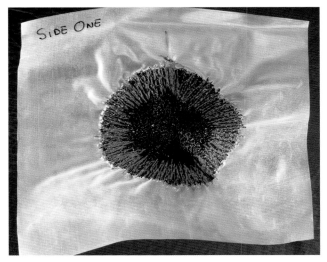

Feathered stitches added only on the edge are shown in red for clarity.

STITCHING A STABLE ROUND BASE

Some projects, such as the vessels, are circular in shape but require a firm, stable round base. A stretched or ruffled edge is not desirable in this instance, so a different initial pattern is used to make a flat form similar to the flat components used for geometric brooches. You'll stitch half the circle at a time, and then turn it clockwise 90° and stitch the next half circle. You'll repeat twice until each quadrant of the circle is covered by four layers of stitching

To stitch a stable round base:

1. Draw a circle onto the stabilizer and then draw perpendicular lines through the center. Number the lines as shown.

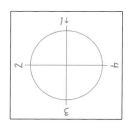

Mark and label stabilizer.

2. Referring to the stitching guide at right, start at the top of the circle and stitch a narrow zigzag stitch over the line marked with the numbers 1 and 3. End the stitching at the bottom of the circle. Move to the left the width of the zigzag stitch and zigzag stitch in a straight line back to the top. Repeat this pattern until the left side of the circle is filled in with zigzag stitches.

3. For ease in stitching using a front-to-back motion, rotate the circle clockwise 90° so the number 2 is at the top. Stitch parallel rows of zigzag stitches on the left half of the circle as before.

4. Rotate the circle clockwise again so the number 3 is at the top. Stitch parallel rows of zigzag stitches on the left half of the circle.

5. Rotate the circle clockwise again so the number 4 is at the top. Stitch parallel rows of zigzag stitches on the left half of the circle.

6. Repeat steps 2–5 as specified in the project instructions.

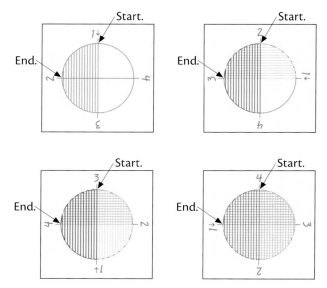

Stitching guide for a stable round base

Completing the Project

When the stitching is complete, remove the stabilizer from the project, and then shape the work and allow it to dry. After drying, the piece can be embellished if desired (see "Beads and Decorative Thread Embellishments" on page 55). Jewelry with individual components will need to be secured together and finished with the appropriate jewelry findings (see "Jewelry Findings" on page 14).

REMOVAL OF STABILIZER

To remove the stabilizer, first trim the excess stabilizer as close as possible to the edge of the project. Then plunge the project into a container of lukewarm water and agitate slightly. Gently rub the edges of the project to make sure the stabilizer has been removed and won't show as a white film after the item is dry. It's nearly impossible—and unnecessary, for most projects—to remove all of the stabilizer. The remaining solution won't show in the body of the piece and will actually help hold the work in the desired shape, particularly on less-dense pieces. Gently squeeze the excess water out of the thread piece, roll it in a towel, and then squeeze to remove even more water.

SHADING

Even though you achieve some shaping on the sewing machine through your selection of stitches, you may see unexpected forms emerging while the piece is wet. Some pieces that initially seemed uninteresting can be manipulated, redesigned, and rejuvenated at this stage. All manner of bending, bowing, pleating, and folding is possible—and if you're unhappy with your results, flatten the shaped piece and try again. For jewelry projects, such as brooches with multiple components, experiment with combining elements into a pleasing design by shaping the pieces and fitting them together.

Once you've "sculpted" the item to your satisfaction, put it on a cooling rack used for baked goods to dry. This shortens drying time by allowing air to circulate under the piece. If your piece involves multiple components, place the individual shapes on the rack to dry. Precise shaping can be maintained by clipping curves to the rack using regular or miniature clothespins, but don't use any clips that might leave a rust stain on the work. Pieces may be left to dry for several hours or overnight at room temperature. If they're secured to the rack, it may be moved outdoors in the sun for quicker drying. To dry them even more quickly, use a hair dryer, but don't try to proceed with any finishing techniques (such as beading, assembling, or gluing) until all components are completely dry. In the event that the shape isn't pleasing or pieces don't fit together as desired, you may wet the pieces again and reshape them.

Scraps of stabilizer that have been trimmed from the edges may be dissolved in a small amount of water to create a stiffener. To add body to a design or help a piece hold its desired shape, wet the piece with water, and then brush on the glue-like solution of dissolved stabilizer while the piece is wet.

If not enough thread layers have been stitched on the work and it's flimsy when dry, it's possible to add more stitching. Assuming the piece is large enough to put back on the sewing machine safely (that is, your fingers won't be too close to the needle) and it does not need to be enlarged, it isn't necessary to use additional stabilizer because you can add stitches to those already in place. Just continue to stitch as in the beginning stages and check the density frequently by holding the work up to a light source until it's thick enough to hold the shape desired. If the piece is small, such as a component of a brooch, the dry work should be placed on a larger piece of stabilizer and tacked down carefully before the stitching process is resumed. When there are enough layers of thread, remove the stabilizer and proceed as though it was the first time.

FINISHING

When completely dry, the piece is ready to be embellished, and any design with multiple components, such as jewelry, is ready to be assembled. If there are any stray threads protruding from the piece, clip them off close to the stitching. There is no need to fasten such threads, as the work isn't going to unravel or fall apart.

The easiest way to assemble jewelry pieces, if the shapes allow, is to position the dry pieces under the needle of the sewing machine and use a closely spaced zigzag stitch as a tacking stitch (put in three or four stitches without moving the work). This technique doesn't work as well if more than three layers are stacked. When assembling more layers, it's best to tack them together in sets of two and then hand tack through all the sets. For the multilayer flower brooch on page 22, it works well to tack the layers in sets of two, and then hot-glue the two sets together when the pin back or stickpin is glued on.

JEWELRY FINDINGS

In jewelry making, the term "findings" refers to the many different pieces of hardware that may be needed to complete and assemble a piece of jewelry. These include the pins that go on the backs of brooches, the part of the earring that attaches to the ear, jump rings, and many other specialty items, such as headpins and bead bars.

Pin backs are designed to be attached by stitching through small holes in the base. However, the thickness and firmness of sculpted-threads brooches makes them very difficult to stitch through, so the backs are attached using hot glue instead. A small amount of the glue will ooze through the holes, helping the stability of the attachment. Stickpins with pads of different sizes can also be glued to the backs of brooches.

Glue the pin back slightly above the center of the brooch so that the brooch won't be top-heavy when worn.

Earring findings are available in pierced and clip-on types and may dangle or be stationary. They include posts, earring hooks, and earring wires. Some clip-on findings have a decorative ball above the loop where the jump ring attaches the drop portion of the earring; others have a slim bar that gives the appearance of a pierced earring. A button-style earring is stationary on the lobe of the ear. Findings for that type have a pad to which you glue the earring.

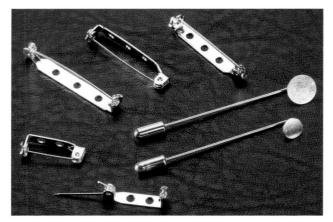

Pin backs and stickpins are available in a range of metal colors and sizes.

Stationary earring findings with pads are available in both pierced and clip-on styles.

Earring wearers all seem to have their favorite type of earring finding, whether post, wire, hook, or clip. All these types are available with loops that can be joined to a jump ring, which connects with the decorative sculpted-threads piece to create an earring that will dangle.

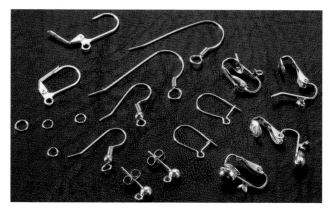

Earring findings with loops for attaching jump rings and creating dangles are available in many styles.

Accordion-pleated earrings can be threaded onto bead bars or headpins (see "Accordion-Pleated Diamond Earrings" on page 33). Bead bars have a ball that unscrews from the bar at one end. The opposite side of the ball has a loop that secures to the earring finding with a jump ring. Headpins may have a decorative end, or the end may be flat like a straight pin, allowing you to thread your own decorative bead into place. Accordion-fold the earring component onto the headpin, and cut the other end to the desired length. Then make a loop at the end with round-nosed pliers. Use a jump ring to connect the loop of the headpin to the earring finding.

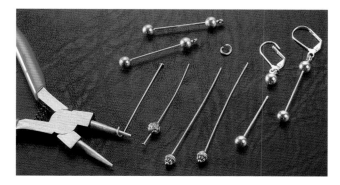

Headpins on the left and bead bars at the top and on the right are ideal for lacing on accordion-pleated sculpted-threads earrings.

Attaching an earring finding can be as easy as gluing it to the back of a sculpted-thread piece. See page 34 for instructions.

Brooches from Geometric Forms

Geometric brooches are a great introduction to sculpted-threads techniques and are relatively easy to make. The brooches are based on square forms, and instructions are also given for triangle shapes. Once you're familiar with the process, try other shapes for an endless variety of brooch designs.

WINGED SQUARES BROOCH
In this bold brooch, lots of visual interest packs into a delightful little accessory.

Winged Squares Brooch

Finished brooches look nice on suits, dresses, jackets, as shawl accents, and even on purses—any place whimsy strikes. The brooches in this chapter are made from flat squares (see "Stitching Flat Forms" on page 10). These are good projects for learning both sculpted-threads techniques and free-motion stitching, plus they're fairly quick to make.

MATERIALS

Refer to "Basic Supplies" on page 8 and "Jewelry Findings" on page 14.

Two 5" squares of stabilizer, each with a 1¾" square drawn in the center

One 5½" square of stabilizer with a 2½" square drawn in the center

One 250-yard spool each of black, red, and white machine-embroidery thread

One 140-yard spool each of black, red, and silver threadlike metallic machine-embroidery thread (not flat foil-type thread)

Jewelry finding for back

Hot-glue gun and glue sticks

Size 14 topstitching or jeans needle

STITCHING CHART

When two different types of thread or two different thread colors are used, you'll need to flip the work over as well as turn it 90° after each layer. Flipping causes the different threads to mix and creates a more interesting effect than solid colors. The stitching chart below explains the order in which to use the threads for each component. Refer to the chart when completing the instructions on pages 18–20.

White component, 1¾" square (middle layer)					
Layer	Stitch Type	Flip	Rotate	Needle Thread	Bobbin Thread
1	Med. zigzag	No	No	White	White
2	Med. zigzag	No	90°	White	White
3	Med. zigzag	No	90°	White	White
4	Med. zigzag	No	90°	White	White
5	Med. zigzag	No	90°	White	White
6	Med. zigzag	No	90°	White	White
7	Med. zigzag	No	90°	White	White
8	Med. zigzag	No	90°	White	White
9	Med. zigzag	No	90°	White	Silver metallic
10	Med. zigzag	Yes	90°	White	Silver metallic
11	Med. zigzag	Yes	90°	White	White
12	Med. zigzag	No	90°	White	White
13	Med. zigzag	No	90°	White	White
14	Med. zigzag	No	90°	White	White
Black component, 2½" square (background)					
Layer	Stitch Type	Flip	Rotate	Needle Thread	Bobbin Thread
1	Med. zigzag	No	No	Black	Black
2	Med. zigzag	No	90°	Black	Black
3	Med. zigzag	No	90°	Black	Black
4	Med. zigzag	No	90°	Black	Black
5	Med. zigzag	No	90°	Black	Black metallic
6	Med. zigzag	Yes	90°	Black	Black metallic
7	Med. zigzag	Yes	90°	Black	Silver metallic
8	Med. zigzag	Yes	90°	Black	Silver metallic
9	Med. zigzag	Yes	90°	Black	Black metallic
10	Med. zigzag	Yes	90°	Black	Black metallic
11	Med. zigzag	Yes	90°	Black	Black metallic
12	Med. zigzag	Yes	90°	Black	Black metallic
13	Med. zigzag	Yes	90°	Black	Black
14	Med. zigzag	No	90°	Black	Black

Red component, 1¾" square (front layer)					
Layer	Stitch Type	Flip	Rotate	Needle Thread	Bobbin Thread
1	Med. zigzag	No	No	Red	Red
2	Med. zigzag	No	90°	Red	Red
3	Med. zigzag	No	90°	Red	Red
4	Med. zigzag	No	90°	Red	Red
5	Med. zigzag	No	90°	Red	Red
6	Med. zigzag	No	90°	Red	Red
7	Med. zigzag	No	90°	Black	Red
8	Med. zigzag	Yes	90°	Black	Red
9	Med. zigzag	No	90°	Red	Red metallic
10	Med. zigzag	Yes	90°	Red	Red metallic
11	Med. zigzag	No	90°	Red	Red
12	Med. zigzag	No	90°	Red	Red

INSTRUCTIONS

Refer to "Sculpted-Threads Basics" on page 7 when completing the following steps.

1. Mark the upper-left corner of a 5" square of stabilizer "side 1" and draw an arrow to indicate the stitching direction on that side.

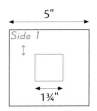

Mark and label stabilizer.

2. Thread the needle and bobbin of the sewing machine with thread, following the chart on page 17 for the white component. Unless the thread is specified as metallic, it's machine-embroidery thread.

3. Using a medium zigzag stitch, stitch over the marked lines of the square on the stabilizer, being sure to pivot at the corners.

4. Starting at the upper-left corner, stitch a line parallel to the left side of the square, directly next to the initial row of stitching. Move the stabilizer to the left the width of the zigzag stitch and stitch back toward the top, staying close to the previous stitching line.

5. When you reach the top border of the square, move the work to the left the width of the zigzag stitch and continue stitching toward the bottom of the square. Repeat in this manner until you reach the right side of the square. The stitching should be even, with no large gaps of stabilizer showing. One "layer" is now complete.

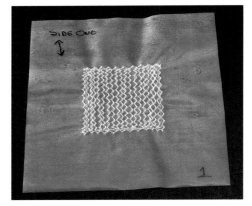

First layer of stitching, with arrow indicating the initial stitching direction

6. With the needle down in either the top or bottom corner of the right side, turn the work 90° and stitch across the first layer of thread in the same manner as before. It does not matter

whether the stitching is done from right to left or left to right.

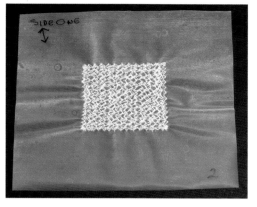

To keep the component flat, the second layer of stitching is made at 90° to the first layer.

7. Continue adding layers of thread to the piece, following the chart on page 17 until you've completed layer 6. Compare your work with the photo below to see if the thread layers have the same amount of coverage. Depending on how close your rows of stitching are, the number of layers needed may vary from the chart. If the thread layers appear too thin, add more layers of stitching until the work resembles the piece in the photo. If the layers appear thicker than in the photo, you can make adjustments in the next step.

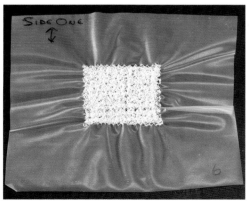

After six layers of stitching, some light is still visible through the element.

8. Continue stitching thread layers in the same manner, following the chart for thread changes and flips until the stabilizer is well covered and no light comes through. If not enough thread is stitched onto the stabilizer, the resulting piece will be flimsy when the stabilizer is removed. If the piece was thicker than the photo after six layers, check for light coming through the piece after layer 12. If it's solid, you may skip the final two layers (13 and 14).

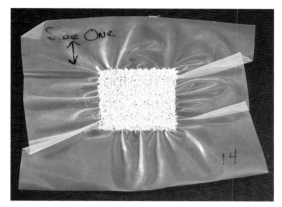

After 14 layers, the component has become dense and will hold its shape.

9. Repeat the process for the black and red components of the design, stitching the layers as described in the stitching chart.

10. Using scissors, make a diagonal cut in the red square starting at one corner and stopping about ¼" from the opposite corner.

Cut.

11. Stitch over the cut edges with a narrow zigzag stitch to finish them. Remove the stabilizer (see "Removal of Stabilizer" on page 13).

12. Shape the components while they're wet, folding over the corner points of the red square using the project photo on page 16 as a guide. Try assembling the pieces to help you visualize where they should be flattened and where they need to bend. After shaping, place the components on a rack to dry. You may use clothespins to help hold the shapes, but don't use clips that can rust.

13. If any of the components are too flimsy to hold their shape after the work is dry, it's possible to add more layers of stitching. If this is necessary, it's best to tack the element onto a larger piece of stabilizer to protect your fingers from the sewing-machine needle while stitching.

14. When all components are dry, it's time to assemble the three parts. You may do this by machine using a "tacking stitch" (a wide zigzag stitch done without moving the work), by hand stitching, or by using a hot-glue gun. Place the white and black squares on point with the white square on top and align the bottom corners. Tack down the white square. Prepare a thread sprig as described on page 61. Position the sprig in the center of the white square and tack it near the bottom corner. Position the red "wings" over the sprig and tack at the side and bottom corners.

15. Finally, secure a pin back or stickpin to the back of the brooch using a hot-glue gun.

Variations on Geometric Forms

Experiment with the following suggestions to add a unique touch to your geometric shapes.

TRIANGLES

Triangles combine nicely with squares as well as rectangles. Stitch them in the same manner as squares (see the Winged Squares Brooch on page 16), with each successive layer stitched at 90° to the previous layer. To maintain flat triangles, stitch down the center from point to base, then move to the left the width of the zigzag stitch, and continue up to the angled side. Move the needle to the left, down the side, and then stitch back down to the base. When one side is filled, stitch across the bottom back to the middle and repeat on the other side. When complete, turn the work 90° and stitch rows parallel to the base. For an example of a triangle component, refer to "Earrings" on page 30.

ALTERING GEOMETRIC FORMS

After the piece is stable, you can alter the stitched components through creative cutting. This might include cutting the middle completely from a square, or cutting two sides of a small square in the center of a larger one and bending back one corner (see the Patriotic Brooch below). Finish the cut edges with a narrow satin stitch, being sure the stitching goes just over the cut edge.

PATRIOTIC BROOCH
Square components and variations of them are layered and staggered for a unique design. A small square was cut and removed from the white component, and two adjacent sides of a square were cut in the red component, which was folded over the blue square and layered over a red-and-blue variegated square. Seed beads and bugle beads are stitched in rows on the red component and randomly over the blue square.

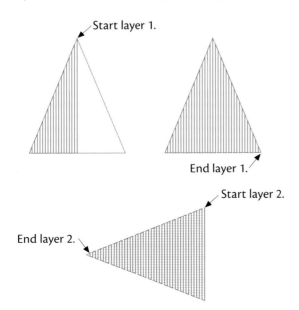

Start layer 1.

End layer 1.

Start layer 2.

End layer 2.

GALLERY

EASY SQUARES BROOCH
Two square elements are butted and stitched together to form a rectangle, and then a square component, layered over a second square set on point, is attached to the center of the rectangle. Looped beading and beaded stamens accent the center (see "Beaded Loops" on page 57 and "Beaded Stamens" on page 56).

ALL BLUES BROOCH
The base component of this piece has fanciful fringed edges, created during the thread-layering process (see "Machine Fringe" on page 62). The narrow embellishment strip has longer fringe and was shaped while wet to create a windswept look. Large beads are scattered in one corner as an accent.

PRIMARY COLORS BROOCH
This design gains dimension from soft folds and rolled edges, which were shaped while the square components were wet. Embellishments consist of scattered beading on the red and green components, covered-edge beading on the blue area, and line beading on the yellowish orange section.

THREE-SQUARED BROOCH
A trio of vibrant squares in graduated sizes received subtle shaping while wet. Then the pieces were set on point and layered, with the bottom points aligned. Thread sprigs with both cut and uncut loops add textural interest between the layers.

Multilayer Flower Brooch

Whether worn as a brooch or pinned to a purse, this project makes a nice accent piece. After learning the technique, experiment with various thread options, such as using a different shade of a single color for each layer of the flower. This project features circular shapes, but the instructions apply to ovals as well.

This four-layer black flower brooch gleams with beaded loops in the center.

MATERIALS

Refer to "Basic Supplies" on page 8 and "Jewelry Findings" on page 14.

One 7" square of stabilizer with a 4" circle drawn in the center

One 6" square of stabilizer with a 3" circle drawn in the center

One 5" square of stabilizer with a 2" circle drawn in the center

Two 4" squares of stabilizer, each with a 1" circle drawn in the center

One 250-yard spool of black machine-embroidery thread

One 250-yard spool of gold metallic machine-embroidery thread

Jewelry finding for back

Hot-glue gun and glue sticks

Size 14 topstitching or jeans needle

STITCHING CHART

Refer to the chart when completing the instructions on page 24.

4" circle (bottom layer)

Layer	Notes	Stitch Type	Flip	Needle Thread	Bobbin Thread
1	128 spokes	Med. zigzag	No	Black	Black
2		Straight	No	Black	Black
3	Outer ¾"	Straight	No	Black	Black
4		Straight	No	Black	Black
5	Outer ½"	Straight	No	Black	Gold metallic
6		Straight	Yes	Black	Gold metallic
7		Straight	No	Black	Black

3" circle (second layer)

Layer	Notes	Stitch Type	Flip	Needle Thread	Bobbin Thread
1	128 spokes	Med. zigzag	No	Black	Black
2		Straight	No	Black	Black
3	Outer ½"	Straight	No	Black	Black
4	Outer ½"	Straight	No	Black	Gold metallic
5		Straight	Yes	Black	Gold metallic
6		Straight	No	Black	Black
7		Straight	No	Black	Black

2" circle (third layer)

Layer	Notes	Stitch Type	Flip	Needle Thread	Bobbin Thread
1	64 spokes	Med. zigzag	No	Black	Black
2		Straight	No	Black	Black
3		Straight	No	Black	Black
4	Outer ½"	Straight	No	Black	Gold metallic
5		Straight	Yes	Black	Gold metallic
6		Straight	No	Black	Black
7		Straight	No	Black	Black

Two 1" circles (top layer)

Layer	Notes	Stitch Type	Flip	Needle Thread	Bobbin Thread
1	64 spokes	Med. zigzag	No	Black	Black
2		Straight	No	Black	Black
3		Straight	No	Black	Black
4		Straight	No	Black	Gold metallic
5		Straight	Yes	Black	Gold metallic
6		Straight	No	Black	Black
7		Straight	No	Black	Black

INSTRUCTIONS

Refer to "Sculpted-Threads Basics" on page 7 when completing the following steps.

1. Stitch the first six layers of thread on the stabilizer with the 4" circle, referring to "Stitching Circular Forms" on page 10 and following the stitching chart on page 23 for directions on the number of spokes to stitch, stitch and thread types, as well as when to flip the stabilizer. After completing layer 6, your work should look similar to the photo below. Avoid stitching the piece too heavily, or the resulting piece will be thick and hard to shape. You can always add more layers of stitching after the stabilizer is removed if the piece seems too flimsy. Complete the stitching on the 4" circle component according to the chart.

After the completion of six stitched layers, the edge begins to ruffle.

2. Make the remaining circle components as indicated in the chart on page 23. When all pieces have been stitched, remove the stabilizer (see "Removal of Stabilizer" on page 13). Shape the pieces, referring to the project photo on page 22, and adjust the fullness on the edges evenly. Place the pieces on a rack to dry.

3. Place the 1" circles wrong sides together, and tack them through the center. If desired, embellish the center with stamens of gold seed beads (see "Beaded Stamens" on page 56).

4. Stack the other three circles right sides up, from largest to smallest, and tack them together through the center.

5. Fold the 1" circles in half and secure them to the center of the layered stack with hot glue. Secure a pin back or stickpin to the back of the flower using a hot-glue gun.

THREAD VARIATIONS TO TRY

- Use two coordinating thread colors, one on each side, throughout.
- Use a metallic and a nonmetallic thread throughout, but flip every round to blend the color and texture.
- Use different colors or types of thread in the bobbin and in the needle. When stitching the rounds only on the edges, flip the stabilizer so the edges are done in the contrasting color.
- Stitch the outer edges only with a contrasting color.
- Start with the darkest or lightest shade of a color and then use progressively lighter or darker shades through the layers.

MIDAS-TOUCHED FLOWER

A lush six-layer flower gains extra drama with gold stitching. The leaf shapes were drawn on stabilizer and stitched from the centerline outward, following the natural pattern of leaf veins. The leaves were folded slightly during shaping. Hot glue holds them to the flower.

ORANGE OVAL FLOWER

A multilayer bloom takes on a different look when ovals are the starting shape instead of circles.

FIERY OVAL FLOWER

Two ovals of the same size are folded and secured atop a larger oval, giving the flower a less-rippled appearance.

CARNATION

A triple-layer flower in white and silver metallic has a light and airy feeling when made with slightly fringed edges (see "Machine Fringe" on page 62).

Magic Circle Brooch

Though this project may look difficult, it's actually easy because you get a lot of help from the combination of circular stitching, stabilizer, and thread. The magic circle technique uses off-center radiating lines of stitches, causing the edges of the circle to stretch and ruffle. The design possibilities are endless and vary with the amount of fullness in the circle.

BLUE RECESS
Twisting of the "magic circle" creates recesses and color changes that practically beg for beaded accents.

MATERIALS

Refer to "Basic Supplies" on page 8 and "Jewelry Findings" on page 14.

One 7" square of stabilizer

One 250-yard spool of variegated machine-embroidery or machine-quilting thread

One 250-yard spool of machine-embroidery thread in a solid coordinating color

One 250-yard spool of metallic machine-embroidery thread (optional)

Jewelry finding for back

Hot-glue gun and glue sticks

Size 16 topstitching needle

INSTRUCTIONS

Refer to "Sculpted-Threads Basics" on page 7 and "Stitching Circular Forms" on page 10 when completing the following steps.

1. Mark the stabilizer according to the diagram, beginning with a 4" circle in the center of the square.

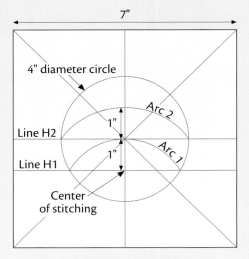

Mark and label stabilizer.

2. Thread the machine with the solid thread and use the variegated thread in the bobbin. Using the small oval at the bottom of the layout as the starting point, begin in the center and complete 128 spokes within the oval. Then stitch two rounds from the center outward for ½". It's important to make sure the center is solid and no light can be seen through it, as it will become impossible to stitch there once the piece ruffles.

The bottom oval has been stitched and the center is completely filled.

3. Stitch around the bottom oval inward from the established edge and overlap the center stitching about ¼" to begin to fill in that area.

4. Starting on the left side, at the intersection of horizontal line H1 and arc 1, stitch between the arc 1 and arc 2 lines to the right side and then back across to the left side, ending at the intersection of line H2 and arc 2.

Two layers of stitching have been completed between the arc 1 and arc 2 lines.

5. Starting at the intersection of H2 and arc 2, stitch from the arc 2 line inward and overlap the small oval (step 2) by ¼". Continue around the bottom half of the piece, stitching as far into the center as possible, and end the stitching at the starting point.

6. Starting at the intersection of H2 and arc 2, stitch out to the upper curve of the circle (between arc 2 and the top). Continue stitching around the bottom half of the piece, stitching as far into the center as possible, and end the stitching at the starting point.

Stitching has begun between the arc 2 line and the top edge of the circle. Notice how solid the rest of the piece is becoming.

7. Starting at the left side at H2 and arc 2, stitch completely around the piece two more times, stitching as far into the center as possible. As the piece begins to ruffle more, it is impossible to stitch all the way to the center.

8. Stitch from the outer edge inward about ½" all around the piece. Stitching on the outer edge causes the ruffling to increase.

9. Repeat step 6. As the ruffles increase, stop periodically and reposition the extra fullness by folding it up and holding it out of the way so that you're stitching in a flat area.

Folding the fullness upward creates a "handle."

10. Repeat steps 8 and 9 until the stabilizer begins to bulge over the edge of the piece. As this happens, hold the stabilizer taut by pulling the edge outward and avoid stitching on that doubled portion. When you cannot pull it out enough to continue stitching, stop and trim away the stabilizer.

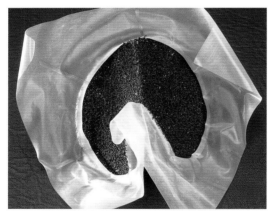

The stabilizer is trying to fold back onto the body of the piece.

11. Check for fullness by folding the piece in half as shown at right. The closer the two folded edges are to each other, the more twists you'll be able to put into your magic circle and the more variation your design will have. If the edges overlap, that's even better.

12. Unfold the piece and continue stitching the outer ½" to ¾", placing the rows of stitches very close together as you go around. It may be easier to stitch only the top portion above line H2 as you pinch up the smaller bottom and use

it for a handle. Go over the edge as you stitch, because this will make the edge firm and nicely finished. Check the fullness often by folding the piece in half. If you wish, do a final round of stitching with metallic thread in the bobbin to add some highlights.

13. Remove the stabilizer (see "Removal of Stabilizer" on page 13). Shape the magic circle as desired and let dry on a wire rack.

14. Attach a pin back to the back of the brooch with a hot-glue gun.

After trimming the stabilizer from the edge, check for fullness by folding the piece in half. Note that this sample is meant to show the shape only, not color placement.

After additional layers of stitching, the folded edges overlap. Compare this to the piece shown above where the folded edges don't meet.

MAGIC CIRCLE BROOCH

CRUSTED WITH BEADS
The folded edges just meet on this piece, which has metallic highlights and heavy beading.

DOUBLE SPIRALS
One of the overlapped folded edges of this brooch was cut from the outside edge to the center, allowing for a double twist. Branched and looped beading is tucked into the recesses.

COOL SYMMETRY
The folded edges of this piece didn't quite meet, but it shapes nicely into a symmetrical brooch.

AQUA SWIRL
More fullness allows for more than one curving element in the finished piece.

Earrings

Earrings created with the sculpted-threads technique are ideal jewelry pieces as they're lightweight, can be made quickly, and offer unlimited design possibilities. The brooch techniques can be adapted for earrings by simply constructing the components in miniature (see "Brooches from Geometric Forms" on page 16 and "Multilayer Flower Brooch" on page 22), so those designs won't be covered again in this section. Provided below are instructions for making earrings constructed from a simple diamond template, as well as for making pillow-style square earrings.

Square pillow-style earrings are made from square components by folding the four corners to the center on the back and tacking in place.

Hoop earrings, accordion-pleated versions, and triangles can all be created using a long, narrow diamond template.

Earrings from Diamonds

Several earring variations can be achieved using a long, narrow diamond-shaped template. You can fold the diamond in half to form a hoop, or accordion-pleat it onto a bead bar or headpin for a textural piece. Triangle-shaped dangles can be made using the top half of the diamond template. All these pieces are done flat. The earrings can be made in either clip-on or pierced styles.

MATERIALS

Refer to "Basic Supplies" on page 8 and "Jewelry Findings" on page 14.

One 5" x 7" piece of stabilizer for hoop or accordion-pleated earrings *or* one 4" x 5" piece of stabilizer for triangles

One 250-yard spool of variegated machine-embroidery thread

One 140-yard spool of variegated metallic machine-embroidery thread in a coordinating color

Jewelry findings:

Two earring findings

Two jump rings

Two bead bars or headpins (for accordion-pleated earrings only)

Two fold-over crimps (for hoop earrings or triangle dangles)

Size 14 topstitching or jeans needle

INSTRUCTIONS

Refer to "Sculpted-Threads Basics" on page 7. Follow each construction step for both earrings before proceeding to the next construction step, to keep the earrings as much alike as possible. Thread the variegated thread in the machine and use the metallic thread in the bobbin. Flip the work after completing each layer to distribute the threads evenly on each side of the earrings.

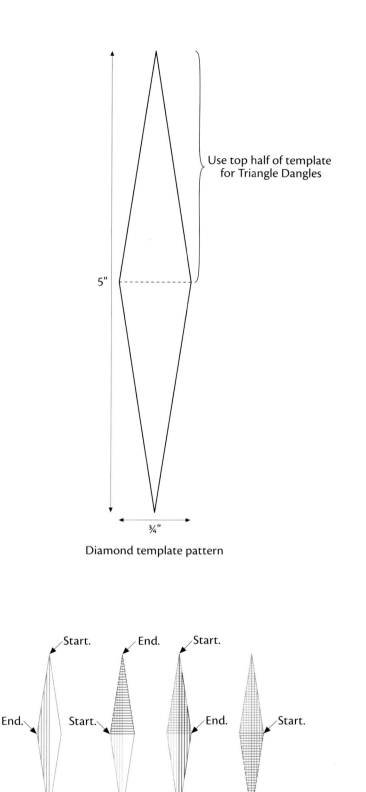

Use top half of template for Triangle Dangles

5"

¾"

Diamond template pattern

Start.   End.   Start.

End.   Start.   End.   Start.

End.

1   2   3   4

Diamond stitching guide

HOOP EARRINGS

1. Trace the diamond template pattern on page 31 twice onto a 5" x 7" piece of stabilizer.

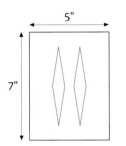

Draw 2 diamonds on the stabilizer.

2. Set your sewing machine for a narrow zigzag stitch and stitch over the marked outline of each diamond. Switch to a straight stitch and, following the stitching lines in diagram 1 of the diamond stitching guide on page 31, begin stitching at the top point of the diamond and continue down the middle to the opposite point. Move one stitching line to the left, along the lower-left outline of the diamond, and stitch straight upward parallel to the first row of stitching until you meet the upper-left outline of the diamond. Move to the left as before and stitch back down to meet the edge of the diamond. Stitch on the outline in an upward motion until the stitching is about the same width away from the previous row. Continue to stitch parallel rows in the same manner until you reach the outer midpoint of the left side.

3. Following the lines in diagram 2 of the stitching guide, start stitching from the midpoint of the left side across to the midpoint of the right side. Then stitch up along the outline of the diamond the width of one stitching line and back across to the left side, stitching parallel lines in the same manner as in step 2. Continue this pattern to the top of the diamond, being sure to stitch over the original outline stitching. You may turn the work so that you're stitching in a forward-and-backward motion, or you may stitch in a horizontal motion without turning the piece.

4. Following the lines in diagram 3 of the diamond stitching guide, stitch on the right half of the diamond in the same manner as in step 2, ending at the outer midpoint on the right side.

5. Following the lines in diagram 4 of the diamond stitching guide, start at the midpoint of the diamond on the right side and stitch parallel lines on the bottom half of the diamond as in step 3. Continue to complete the first layer of stitching on the diamond.

6. Repeat the stitching pattern for the diamond three more times. When you hold the diamonds to the light, you should see some openness, as these pieces are meant to be airy and light.

7. Remove the stabilizer (see "Removal of Stabilizer" on page 13). Place the diamonds flat on a rack and let dry.

8. Finish the earrings by attaching a fold-over crimp, jump ring, and earring finding (see "Finishing Earrings" on page 33).

ACCORDION-PLEATED DIAMOND EARRINGS

Follow steps 1–7 of "Hoop Earrings" on page 32, repeating the stitching pattern for two additional thread layers in step 6. Finish the earrings by pleating and threading them onto a bead bar or headpin (see "Finishing Earrings" at right.

TRIANGLE DANGLES

On a 4" x 5" piece of stabilizer, trace half of the diamond template pattern, as indicated on page 31, twice. Refer to "Triangles" on page 20 for stitching a triangle flat form. Stitch four times in each direction to produce a stable triangle. Remove the stabilizer (see "Removal of Stabilizer" on page 13). Place the triangles flat on a rack to dry. Finish the earrings by attaching a fold-over crimp, jump ring, and earring finding (see "Finishing Earrings" at right).

FINISHING EARRINGS

Refer to "Jewelry Findings" on page 14 and the instructions below for finishing earrings.

Attaching a crimp. On both the hoop earrings and the triangle dangles, a fold-over crimp finding, which has a loop on one end, is attached to the tip of the earring piece. A jump ring connects the loop on the crimp to the earring finding. For security, add a drop of clear cement or nail polish to the top of the thread piece before attaching the crimp. To attach a crimp, insert the pointed end of the triangle or the pointed ends of the folded diamond into the open side of the crimp. Close securely with crimping pliers.

Closing the fold-over crimp with pliers

Attaching a jump ring. A small split ring called a jump ring connects earring findings to other hardware. To open the jump ring, use two pairs of pliers to twist the ends in opposite directions. Never pull the ends straight apart, as that will weaken and break or distort the jump ring. Thread the loops of the fold-over crimp and the earring finding onto the opened jump ring and then close it in the same manner that you opened it, realigning the ends so there is no gap.

A jump ring connects the fold-over crimp to the earring finding.

Using bead bars and headpins. For accordion-pleated earrings, fold the diamond in half to find the center and fan-fold one side, keeping the folds the same size. Push an awl through the center of the folds to spread the threads apart. Continue to fan-fold the remaining half of the diamond in the same manner and insert the awl through the center of those folds.

An awl is used to spread the threads so that a bead bar or headpin can be inserted through the folds.

Remove the awl and insert the bead bar or headpin into the holes. If using a headpin, finish the end by making a loop, using round-nose pliers. Connect the loop at the top of the bead bar or headpin to the earring finding using a jump ring if necessary (see "Attaching a jump ring" on page 33).

Square Pillow Earrings

A 1½" square is stitched flat and shaped by tacking the corners together by hand. An earring finding is glued to the back.

Square hollow earrings resembling pillows can be made in both pierced and clip-on styles.

To make these earrings, draw a pair of 1½" squares on a 5" square of stabilizer. Follow the instructions for the Winged Squares Brooch on pages 16–19, steps 1–7, stitching only four layers of thread (a multicolored flat metallic and coordinating multicolored machine-embroidery thread were used for this project). The piece should be airy but stable enough to hold its shape. Remove the stabilizer (see "Removal of Stabilizer" on page 13). Place the squares flat on a rack and let dry. Finish the earrings by folding the four corners of the square to the center on the back, tacking them together by hand with a needle and thread. Using a hot-glue gun and glue sticks, attach an earring finding with a pad just above the center on the back of each square.

DANGLING SQUARES
A bail finding is the suitable solution for turning a 1" square into a dangling earring.

PLEATED DROPS
A ⅜" x 7" strip is stitched with layers of thread, and then pleated and placed on a headpin with a decorative beaded end.

FLOWER STUDS
A 1½"-diameter circle (see "Stitching Circular Forms" on page 10) is hot-glued to an earring finding with a pad.

Undersea Forms

Undersea forms are pure fantasy, offering unlimited opportunities to explore shape, color, and embellishment. Depending on the fullness of the outer edge, you can mold just a few ruffles or many. This is a chance to try blending, using shades of a single color or making transitions from light to medium to dark with different colors. After stitching every few layers, remove the form from the machine and experiment with the ruffles. Don't be afraid to twist and turn the form to bring out symmetrical or asymmetrical designs. For this piece to hold its shape, it needs to be heavily stitched and stiff. Because the piece won't become any stiffer when the stabilizer is removed, it's important to continue stitching until you're certain the shape is firm.

GOLDEN RUFFLES
Three shades of yellow create a cheery, playful mix in this ruffled undersea form.

MATERIALS

Refer to "Basic Supplies" on page 8.

One 12" square of heavyweight water-soluble stabilizer

Machine-embroidery thread in light, medium, and dark shades of the same color family *or* three coordinating colors that are light, medium, and dark. You'll need approximately 1,500 yards of thread total to complete the form.

Size 16 or 18 topstitching or jeans needle

Beads for embellishment (optional)

INSTRUCTIONS

Refer to "Sculpted-Threads Basics" on page 7 when completing the following steps.

1. Draw a 9" circle in the middle of the 12" square of stabilizer, and then draw a 2½" circle in the center of the 9" circle. Draw perpendicular lines through the center of the circles and mark one line with an arrow outside the circle to indicate the starting point.

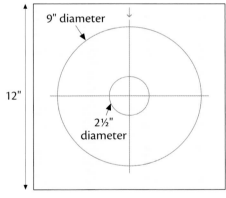

Mark and label stabilizer.

2. Thread the machine, both top and bobbin, with the light thread color and set the machine to a medium zigzag stitch. Stitch 64 spokes within the 9" circle.

3. The center (2½") circle will begin to rise up and needs to be flattened at this point. Begin by stitching on the outline for the 2½" circle with a straight stitch while easing the spokes flat. Continue to stitch in a spiral pattern into the center.

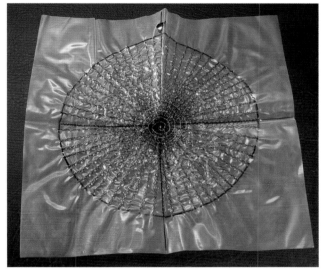

The circle has been stitched with 64 spokes, and spiral stitching has been used in the center to flatten that area. Contrasting thread colors are shown in this sample for clarity.

4. Switch to a medium zigzag stitch and stitch over the center using horizontal and then vertical lines to flatten and firm that area. Continue until no light is visible through the work.

5. Using the medium zigzag stitch, add spokes between the original 64 spokes in the area from the 2½" circle outward to the 9" circle. This will increase the number of spokes to 128.

6. Stitch from the outer edge (9" circle) inward for 1", spacing the lines close to each other.

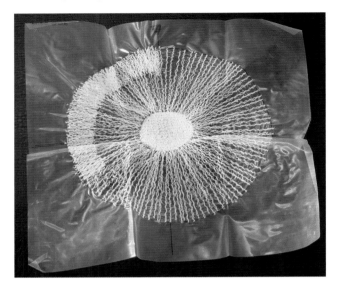

A total of 128 spokes have been stitched on the circle. The center circle has been densely stitched to flatten it, and the 1" border around the outer edge is partially completed.

7. Stitch between the 2½" and 9" circles, filling in that area with even rows of radiating stitching. Work on one quadrant at a time and overlap the center circle by ¼" to prevent a soft spot from forming. Be sure the stitching is even so that ruffles will form evenly. Areas of thin stitching will appear as dimples and should be removed by adding thread in that area and blending into thicker areas on each side. Continue stitching the radiating lines in this area until the work feels firm and no light is shining through.

The radiating lines between base and edge have been started on the lower left quadrant of the circle and are complete on the upper right quadrant.

8. Thread the needle with medium-colored thread and leave the light-colored thread in the bobbin. Change to a straight stitch and continue to stitch as in step 7, keeping the stitching even across the surface. Feather the medium color into the light color at the edge of the center circle by varying where the medium color stops, stitching some lines longer and some shorter. Flip the work over after each thread layer to help blend and shade the colors. Repeat this until the piece is stiff and will hold the ruffles upright.

9. Change the needle thread to the dark color and the bobbin thread to the medium color. Stitch only on the outer 1" and feather the darker color into the medium color. Flip the work after each thread layer as in step 8 to further blend and shade. For a nicely finished edge, cut away the stabilizer at the stitching line and then stitch a couple of rounds that continue over the edge.

10. Remove the stabilizer (see "Removal of Stabilizer" on page 13). Shape into graceful curves and flatten as necessary so it will sit solidly. Place on a rack to dry.

11. If desired, embellish the form with beads (see "Beads and Decorative Thread Embellishments" on page 55).

UNDERSEA FORMS

GALLERY

UNDERWATER SUNSHINE
*This radiant undersea form shows off beaded edges,
as well as pools of beads stitched in the center.*

SEA-COLORED FORM
*The fuller the edge becomes, the more ruffles can be
formed and the less open the form will be.*

RUFFLES EVERY WHICH WAY
*The ruffles in this undersea form were given an
asymmetrical attitude by shaping them while wet.*

Shallow Vessel

A shallow thread vessel makes a striking decorator piece. Embellish with beads, accent with fringe or contrasting stitching, or leave it as is when you've finished stitching. These instructions are for a small vessel, but you could make one in any size using the same basic techniques. Two threads, a variegated and a solid, are used for this shallow bowl, but you could instead select more thread colors and use blending and shading as described in "Undersea Forms" on page 36.

BOWL OF BASIC COLORS
The starburst pattern on this vessel was added by turning the bowl over and stitching a radiating design in the center. This allowed the variegated thread that was used in the bobbin to create a pattern on the inside of the bowl.

MATERIALS

Refer to "Basic Supplies" on page 8.

One 9" square of heavyweight water-soluble stabilizer

Variegated machine-embroidery thread, approximately 800 yards

Solid-color machine-embroidery thread in a coordinating shade, approximately 800 yards

Beads for embellishing (optional)

Size 16 or 18 topstitching or jeans needle

INSTRUCTIONS

Refer to "Sculpted-Threads Basics" on page 7 when completing the following steps.

1. Draw a 7"-diameter circle in the middle of the 9" square of stabilizer, and then draw a 5" circle in the center of the 7" circle. Draw perpendicular lines through the center of the circles and mark one line with an arrow outside the circle to indicate the starting point. Number the lines as shown.

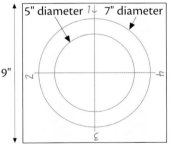

Mark and label stabilizer.

2. Thread the variegated thread in the bobbin and the solid-color thread in the needle and begin stitching inside the 5" circle with a narrow zigzag stitch, following the instructions for "Stitching a Stable Round Base" on page 12.

3. Continue the stitching for a stable round base until each of the four sections has been stitched four times, resulting in eight layers of thread in each section. The piece will not be solid and some light can be seen through it at this point.

4. Switch to a straight stitch and, starting in the center, stitch a radiating pattern out about 1".

As this stitching is done, the edge will start to ripple. Control this and flatten the piece by sewing concentric circles from the radiating stitches to the outer edge of the 5" circle.

For clarity, contrasting thread was used on this sample to show the radiating stitches at the center and the concentric circles that flatten out the edge.

5. Stitch a 1" border of radiating stitches around the radiating stitches in the center, overlapping the center stitches by about ¼". Stitch additional concentric circles around the outer edge to keep the base flat.

As more radiating stitches are added (shown in pale yellow thread for clarity), additional concentric circles are also stitched to keep the base flat.

6. Continue alternating the two stitch patterns until only the last ¾" of the original 5" circle remains unstitched.

7. Stitch a band around the 7" circle by using a straight stitch and short strokes of back-and-forth stitches. The band should start on the line and continue outward about ⅜" to ½". As this stitching is done, ease in the fullness of the stabilizer by pinching it in little pleats and stitching over them.

8. Hold the unstitched area between the base and the banded edge taut and stitch widely spaced lines between the base and the banded edge. The combination of the easing in step 7 and the stitching on the sides will shape the vessel.

The sides of the vessel begin to take shape with the short back-and-forth stitches that form the outer band and the widely spaced lines between circles. Variegated thread was used in the needle for steps 6–8 for clarity.

9. Continue to stitch lines on the sides as in step 8, gradually easing in the fullness. As this is done, the edge, which started out nearly straight upright, will begin to flare out and the shape can be lost. To prevent this, alternate the stitching layers on the sides with short strokes of back-and-forth stitches parallel to the outer edge as in step 7. This helps to pull the sides back in and eliminate the flare. As the stitching

progresses, there will be less stabilizer to hold onto. If it's difficult to grasp the edge, you may wish to stitch strips of additional stabilizer to the original square (see "Stabilizer" on page 9). Be sure to ease in the fullness when doing this.

Extra stabilizer has been stitched to the edges of the original square. This sample was made with mostly yellow thread on the left and has been left unfinished on that side to show how the piece flares out. The right side, stitched with variegated thread, shows how the sides turn upright when strokes of back-and-forth stitching are added to the sides. The yellow parallel stitches started on the rim (shown in the bottom left of the photo) will tighten up the left side and pull it upright when completed.

10. Continue to stitch until the vessel is smooth with sides that turn upward, and the vessel supports itself. Decorative stitching can be done by turning the piece inside out and adding some radiating lines. The lines will appear variegated on the solid-colored side of the vessel (see the project photo on page 40).

11. Remove the stabilizer (see "Removal of Stabilizer" on page 13). Shape the vessel, being sure that the bottom is smooth (see "Shaping" on page 13). Place on a rack to dry.

12. Embellish the edges with seed beads (see "Beaded Edges" on page 60).

FRINGED BOWL
A small vessel makes a big impression with scattered beading in the bottom, beading on the edge, and a crowning touch of branched-beaded fringe.

SEA SPRAY
This charming bowl has a rim of delicate-looking thread fringe, which was stitched with the sewing machine before the stabilizer was removed (see "Machine Fringe" on page 62).

SOMETHING WENT ASKEW
Sometimes it's fun to sculpt a free-form shape. The many thread colors and beaded accents add to the whimsy of this bright piece.

High-Sided Vessel

This bowl-shaped vessel with high sides is created by alternating between two stitching patterns—one that increases the size of the piece and one that shapes the sides. The project instructions that follow call for different thread colors in the bobbin and the needle, and the piece is flipped throughout the stitching to blend the colors and let them provide an interesting effect. Like the shallow vessel, this project could be made using different-colored threads on each side of the bowl.

MEMORIES FROM IRELAND
The flared top on this tall vessel provides the perfect opportunity for a simple zigzag beading design.

MATERIALS

Refer to "Basic Supplies" on page 8.

One 18" square of heavyweight stabilizer (See "Stabilizer" on page 9 for piecing if using a narrower material.)

Two different machine-embroidery threads: they may be a metallic and a nonmetallic, two different colors, or two shades of one color. You'll need approximately 2,200 yards total.

Size 16 or 18 topstitching or jeans needle

INSTRUCTIONS

Refer to sculpted-Threads Basics" on page 7 and the stitching guide on page 48 when completing the following steps.

1. Draw a 4"-diameter circle in the middle of the 18" square of stabilizer. Draw concentric circles spaced 1" apart around the 4" circle, with the final one measuring 14" in diameter. Draw perpendicular lines through the center of the circles and mark one line with an arrow to indicate the starting point. Number the lines as shown.

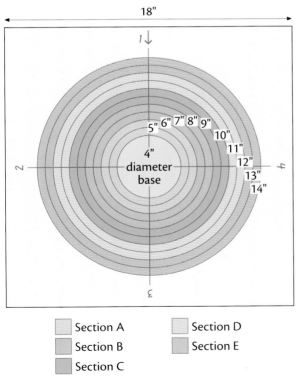

Section A   Section D
Section B   Section E
Section C

2. Thread the machine with one thread and use a different thread in the bobbin. Make a stable round base within the 4" circle, referring to "Stitching a Stable Round Base" on page 12. Repeat steps 2–5 of that section five times to form the base for the high-sided vessel.

3. Change to a straight stitch and flip the stabilizer over so the colors are reversed. Stitch 64 spokes (see "Stitching Circular Forms" on page 10), starting in the center of the base with the ends radiating out to the 5"-diameter line. Continue with the next 64 spokes, radiating out to the 6"-diameter line.

Formation of the sides begins with spokes stitched outward from the center. The right side of the sample shows the first round of spokes radiating out to the 5" line, and the left side shows a partially completed second round of spokes radiating out to the 6" line.

4. Begin to shape the sides by stitching back and forth in ½" intervals on the 5" line while easing in the stabilizer. Keep the stabilizer taut between the center and the stitching line to help form small tucks for easing.

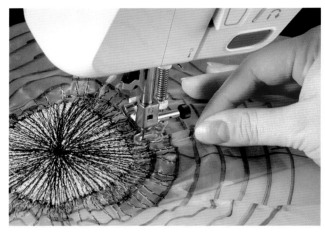

The ends of the spokes are eased closer together by stitching on the 5" line, while the stabilizer is pinched together to form small tucks (orange thread is used for clarity). Easing helps the sides turn upright.

5. Repeat the easing technique from step 4 on the 6" line of the stabilizer. The sides should be at a 90° angle to the base.

After easing along the 5" and 6" circles, the sides of the vessel begin to hold their shape.

6. Firm up the sides by stitching the same back-and-forth stitches from step 4 between the 4" and 6" lines to fill them in. Maintain tension on the stabilizer as it's being stitched, so the area condenses without pulling the parallel lines closer together. The heavier the stitching is in this step, the more upright the sides will be. There will be some unavoidable stretching when the radiating stitches are added in the next step, but denser stitches now will help minimize stretching later.

The area between the easing rows has been completely filled in and is ready for the next step.

7. Turn the work over so that the colors are reversed, and stitch a round of stitches ½" long that go above and below the 4" line. This round will prevent a weak place at the junction of the radiating stitches and the parallel stitches.

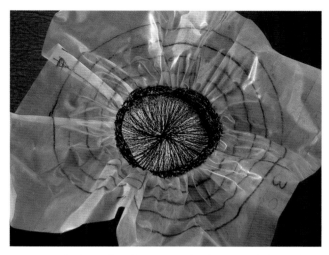

A round of stitches between the base and the sides (shown in orange for clarity) strengthens the junction.

8. Starting near the center of the base, stitch a round of radiating lines outward to the 6" line. How close to the center you start depends on the thickness that has already been established. Radiating stitches should be spaced evenly so that ruffles don't form. Stitch several rounds as necessary to cover section A, checking the density by holding the work to a light source after each round. When you can no longer see stabilizer through the thread, it's time to begin work on the next section.

The radiating stitches from the center of the base up to the edge (shown in orange) add more firmness to the sides.

9. Begin construction of section B by stitching radiating lines starting about ½" inside the 4" line and continuing out to the 7" line. The ends of the radiating lines should be spaced about ½" apart on the 7" line. Keep the stabilizer taut so the circle lines don't pull closer together. If pleats form, stitch through them. Repeat the radiating stitches out to the 8" line, placing them between the stitches of the previous round.

Radiating lines, shown in orange, are stitched to the 7" and then 8" lines.

10. Shape the sides in section B by stitching back and forth in ½" intervals on the 7" and then the 8" line, while easing in the stabilizer as before.

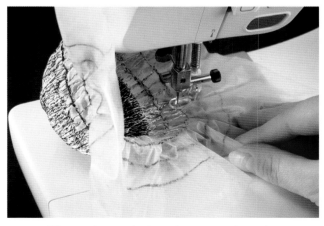

The easing technique is repeated on the 7" and 8" lines (shown in orange thread).

11. Continue stitching back and forth in ½" intervals between the 7" and 8" lines to fill the area with stitching. Keep the stabilizer taut so the area condenses without pulling the parallel lines together.

12. Continue as in steps 9–11 for the next three sections, referring to the stitching guide below. Use the 9" and 10" lines for section C, the 11" and 12" lines for section D, and the 13" and 14" lines for section E. Be sure that the section closest to the center is firm and will stand upright before you proceed to a new section. Since construction is done across two sections at a time, the section farther from the center will receive additional radiating stitches as the construction progresses. Note: For a flared effect on the top edge, *do not* stitch a row of parallel stitches between the 13"- and 14"- diameter lines. This allows the edge to stretch slightly and flare.

13. Remove the stabilizer (see "Removal of Stabilizer" on page 13). Shape the vessel, making sure the bottom is smooth and the piece will sit upright while it's wet. Place on a rack to dry.

14. Embellish the vessel with lines of beads in a zigzag pattern (see "Beaded Lines" on page 59). Use five seed beads in each line before anchoring the thread by sewing it to the underside of the vessel. A contrasting bead should be strung onto the needle on the underside of the vessel before inserting the needle back through to the front. The single bead on the underside adds interest and hides the anchoring stitch.

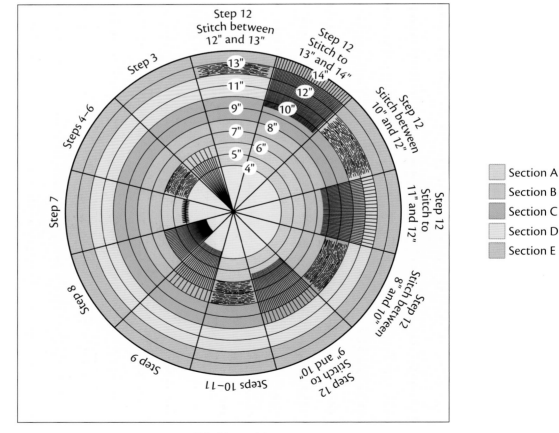

Stitching guide

BLAZING BOWL
Free-form shaping and changes of thread color conjure up the effect of fire in this vessel. The fringe is machine-embroidery thread that was added by hand after the piece was formed and dry (see "Soft Fringe" on page 62).

A J HAWKS VESSEL
Squeezing a plain vessel into a free-form design during the shaping process gave interest to this red-and-blue bowl. Branched fringe (see "Branched Edges" on page 60) done with contrasting tips gives a feeling of motion.

HIGH-SIDED VESSEL

SPRINKLED WITH BLUE
As construction neared the top of this vessel, the edge was eased more tightly so it would cup inward. Beads are placed only on the outside edge to emphasize the inward motion.

ORANGE CUP
The last section of the side was not stitched with the parallel rows of stitching used elsewhere, allowing the edge of this piece to flare out slightly. The covered beaded edge (see "Beaded Edges" on page 60) was done with rust-colored bugle beads and light orange seed beads, resulting in the illusion of little lights in the beading.

Small Bags

A small bag made from a sculpted-threads flat form is handy for carrying a cell phone and keys or a tube of lipstick and credit card. When made with metallic thread, it's a glitzy piece that is sure to get some attention. All three bags shown below are made with a 10" square of "thread fabric." Because the fabric is somewhat delicate, this is meant to be an accent piece rather than a heavy-duty carryall kind of bag.

MATERIALS (FOR ONE BAG)

Refer to "Basic Supplies" on page 8 and bag styles on page 53.

One 14" square of heavyweight water-soluble stabilizer (See "Stabilizer" on page 9 if material isn't 14" wide.)

One 250-yard spool of variegated metallic thread

One 250-yard spool of variegated machine-embroidery thread in a coordinating color

Finishing materials and findings for the Carryout Bag:

1⅝ yards of twisted cord

½" sew-on snap

Finishing materials and findings for the Nosegay Bag:

6 yards of rattail cord

2 decorative ball buttons, ½" in diameter

10" of gold elastic cord, for closure

Clear nail polish or Fray Check

Finishing materials and findings for the Square Bag:

1⅓ yards of chain

4 jump rings, ½" in diameter

Magnetic clasp or snap, for closure

Metal button with shank removed

Size 14 topstitching or jeans needle

INSTRUCTIONS FOR THREAD FABRIC

Refer to "Sculpted-Threads Basics" on page 7 when completing the following steps.

1. On the 14" square of stabilizer, mark a 1" grid. A rotary-cutting mat marked with a grid makes this easy because the lines are visible through the stabilizer. Tape down the corners of the stabilizer and use a ruler and felt-tip marker to draw the lines 1" apart in both directions.

2. Thread the machine with the metallic thread in the bobbin and the machine-embroidery thread in the needle. Leave a 1" border all around and begin stitching with a straight stitch at the upper-right corner, 1" from the edges. Note that you will start by stitching a 12" square, although the finished size of the thread fabric will be 10" square due to shrinking. Stitch to the opposite side, stopping 1" from the edge, and then stitch left across the marked bottom horizontal line to the next vertical line. Stitch back to the top on that line, move to the left, and continue in the

same manner across the entire piece. When all vertical lines have been stitched, turn the stabilizer 90° and repeat the process in the other direction. All grid lines have now been stitched.

3. Flip the stabilizer over, turn it 90°, and stitch in the same manner, this time between each previously stitched line in both directions. The grid is now a ½" pattern.

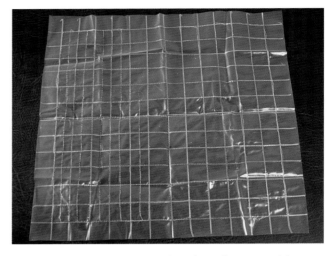

Stitching has been completed on the 1" grid lines in both directions and the next stitching is started between the previous rows of stitching.

4. Flip and turn the work 90° and stitch in both directions between each pair of rows.

5. Continue in the same manner, stitching in straight lines in one direction, then the other direction, and flip. When it isn't possible to stitch between the previous rows, stitch about a needle's width apart. The number of layers you add will depend on how closely you stitch. The piece shouldn't be so solid that it won't bend easily. Light should still be visible through it and the piece should measure 10" square. If one measurement is longer, stitch another layer in that direction to pull it in.

6. Remove the stabilizer (see "Removal of Stabilizer" on page 13) and dry the square flat (see "Shaping" on page 13). If there are wrinkles after it dries, it can be flattened with an iron, but use caution with the metallic threads and place a press cloth on top of the piece before touching it with a hot iron. If edges are very ragged, you can trim them with a rotary cutter. The remaining stabilizer that was in the water during the removal process will hold the stitches together.

Carryout Bag   Nosegay Bag   Square Bag

FOLDING AND FINISHING INSTRUCTIONS FOR THE CARRYOUT BAG

1. With the fabric right side up, fold one corner of the square up 5" so the point aligns with the opposite corner.

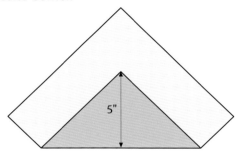

2. Measure in 2¼" from the right edge of the fold line and fold over, keeping the folds aligned at the bottom of the bag. Repeat on the other side.

3. Mark points 1" from the side folds as shown. On each side, fold the side flap back diagonally on a line that connects the marked point to the corner.

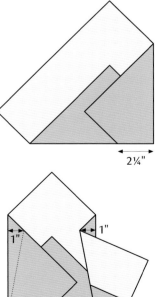

4. Fold the side flaps back toward the bag, creating a new fold on each side that aligns evenly with the side and forms a gusset to allow for expansion.

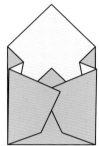

5. Using a hand needle and matching thread, stitch the flaps to the bag along the raw edges.

6. Tack twisted cording to the bag, starting at the point of the flap and leaving a 6" tail. Tack the cording along the edge of the flap, and then along the back fold of the gusset, across the bottom, up the back of the gusset on the opposite side, and along the remaining side of the flap to the point.

7. Trim the cord, leaving a 6" tail. Tie the two tails in an overhand knot close to the point, and sew a large snap to the underside of the knot and to the corresponding position on the bag.

8. Tie an overhand knot 1" from the ends of the cord tails at the center point of the flap and unravel the cord to the knots, forming tassels.

9. On the remaining cord, tie overhand knots in each end so that 1" extends beyond the knot. Untwist this portion to create a tassel on each end.

10. Sew the knots to the top corners of the bag at the back gusset.

FOLDING AND FINISHING INSTRUCTIONS FOR THE NOSEGAY BAG

1. Fold the square in half diagonally so that the top layer is about ¼" inside the bottom layer. Fold the lower edge of the bottom layer over the top layer and stitch close to the raw edge.

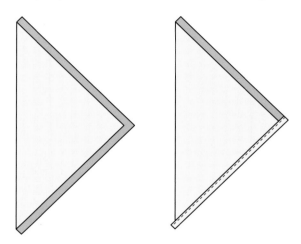

2. Refold the piece, orienting the seam down the center as shown.

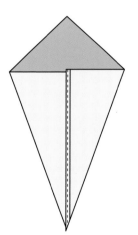

3. Fold the bottom point up 3½" and attach a button to the point, securing it to the front of the bag.

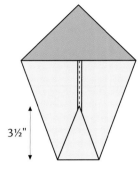

3½"

4. Cut three 2-yard lengths of rattail cord and tie all three lengths together with an overhand knot 4" from the ends. Braid down to 4" from the opposite ends and tie the three cords together in a knot. Tie an overhand knot as close to each cord end as possible and trim off any excess. Seal all cord ends with clear nail polish or Fray Check. Sew the braided cord to the sides of the bag as shown in the project photo on page 51.

5. Sew a decorative ball button to the point of the top flap on the right side.

6. Insert a 6" length of gold elastic cord into the shank of the upper button. Pull the ends down around the lower button and tie an overhand knot in a position to hold the flap down.

FOLDING AND FINISHING INSTRUCTIONS FOR THE SQUARE BAG

1. Fold three corners of the square thread fabric toward the center so that they overlap by ¼", and then stitch by hand along the overlapped edges with matching thread.

2. Attach a magnetic clasp or snap to the back side of the top flap and to the corresponding position under the flap. Glue the decorative button over the hardware on the outside of the flap.

3. Open four ½" jump rings and work them into the corners of the bag (see "Attaching a jump ring" on page 33). Insert the end links of the chain into the lower jump rings and close them. Pull the chain up the side of the bag to the upper corner, insert the jump ring into the nearest link that keeps the chain taut, and close the jump ring. Repeat on the other side.

Beads and Decorative Thread Embellishments

My favorite materials for embellishing sculpted-threads projects are beads and decorative machine-embroidery threads. Beads, in either simple or elaborate patterns, add sparkle and texture to sculpted-threads designs. Seed beads are the most common type used on these pieces, but bugle beads are also used.

Embellishing with beads is done more easily through the thinnest areas of the work, so for designs with multiple components it's best to embellish before assembling the pieces. Use needles small enough to go through the bead, but sturdy enough to penetrate the thread work. Regular beading needles are too delicate for this process, as it's often necessary to push with a thimble or pull with a pair of pliers. The best hand needles are a #11 "straw" or milliner's needle or a #9 or #10 Sharp. Use beading thread that matches the work so it won't show when traveling across the finished piece. Some beading threads are prewaxed, but if in doubt, apply beeswax to your thread. Secure the thread at the beginning and end of the stitching by hiding a knot or by stitching through the work several times in one place.

Thread embellishments, such as decorative fringe edging or a colorful thread sprig, can be added to sculpted-threads projects for textural interest and contrast. Thread sprigs, which are similar to tassels, make great embellishments on brooches.

Beaded Flower Stamens

Flower brooches can be enhanced with beaded stamens, which can be straight, branched, or looped. Branched stamens are similar to straight stamens, but form a Y shape, giving a fuller appearance to the ends. Looped stamens can be long or short for different effects.

BEADED STAMENS

A stamen is a straight line of beads that may stand straight up or fall over depending on how tightly the thread is pulled. Lengths may vary in one application, such as being longer in the center and shorter around the edges. The stamens can all be made of a single color, or the colors can vary through the stamen.

To make stamens, anchor the thread in the sculpted-threads piece, bring the needle to the right side, and string on two to eight beads or more, depending on the desired look. Stitch back through the beads on the thread, skipping the last one threaded, and pull tightly against the base.

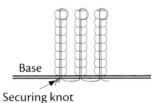

Take a stitch into the project and repeat for as many stamens as desired. When finished, take the thread to the wrong side and anchor securely. Seed beads work best for this, but bugles with seed beads at both ends can be used as well.

Stringing on a contrasting-color bead last gives an interesting effect. The end can also be finished with a loop of matching or contrasting beads by adding three more beads to the stamen before passing the thread back through it.

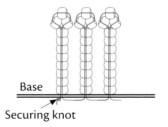

BRANCHED STRANDS

Branched strands can be used to fill a void, such as in the center of a cone shape. Anchor the thread in the sculpted-threads piece, bring it to the right side, and string eight seed beads onto it. Skip the last bead strung and put the needle back through the next three beads.

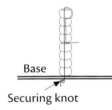

String four additional beads onto the thread, skip the last one, put the needle back through the other three, then back through the remaining four into the base, and anchor securely. Also see "Branched Edges" on page 60.

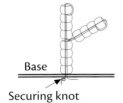

Multibranched strands may be made by using more beads to start with and making two branches before returning to the base as shown in the photo at left.

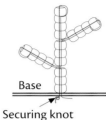

BEADED LOOPS

Loops work best when an odd number of beads are used so that a bead is at the top of the loop rather than having the thread showing between two beads at the top. Anchor the thread in the sculpted-threads piece, bring the needle to the right side, and string 3 to 11 seed beads depending on how long of a loop you want. Insert the needle into the base close to the point where it came out to form a loop of beads.

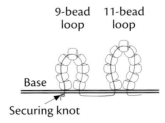

Beaded Surface Embellishments

A touch of beading on the surface often provides the finishing touch to jewelry or a vessel. It can be the difference between "OK" and "wow!"

SCATTERED BEADING

In the scattered-beading technique, beads are stitched one at a time in a random pattern over a surface. For a pleasing overall appearance, create clusters of beads, maintaining an equal distance between each bead in the cluster. Stitched close together, beads have a puddled effect and a greater impact.

To stitch scattered beads, anchor the thread in the sculpted-threads piece, bring the needle to the right side, and string on a single bead. Insert the needle into the base as close to the bead as possible, carry the thread across the base to the next location, and repeat. Be sure the thread passing on the other side isn't visible or detracting. Use small running stitches to travel long distances and they won't be seen if the thread matches the base.

BRANCHED SURFACE BEADING

The branched technique described for flower stamens may also be used on a flat surface. Anchor the thread in the sculpted-threads piece, bring the needle to the right side and string the desired number of beads onto the thread, and then stitch down into the piece at the end of the strung beads. Bring the thread back to the surface at the second bead from the end and proceed back through the beads a second time until reaching the point where a branch is desired. Take a stitch down into the piece and then back up. Thread on the branching beads, insert the needle down into the piece, and back up at the second bead from the end of the branch; proceed back through the beads, exiting at the start of the branch. Take a stitch down and then back. Insert the needle back through the remaining beads as shown. Anchor the thread.

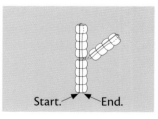

Start.   End.

:::::: Indicates thread traveling on wrong side.

BEADED LINES

This beading embellishment refers to stringing multiple beads (two to six) before anchoring them. They may be anchored in a random pattern, in rows, or in straight, zigzag, curved, or broken lines. Lines may be stitched over each other for a textural effect. When using bugle beads, be sure to string a small seed bead before and after the bugle so that it won't cut the thread (see "Working with Bugle Beads" at right).

Straight lines

Starting anchor

Wide lines

Starting anchor

Irregular lines

Starting anchor

Lines over lines

Starting anchor

····· Indicates thread traveling on wrong side.

WORKING WITH BUGLE BEADS

Bugle beads, which are cylindrical, are sharp on the ends and need to be combined with a small seed bead on each end to protect the thread from being cut.

Seed beads

Bugle bead

BEADED LINES FOLLOWING COLOR PATTERNS

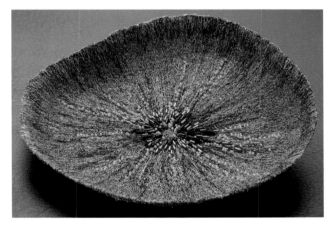

When contrasting machine stitching is done for a decorative effect in the bottom of a vessel, a line of beads in a similar shade can be an effective accent to that stitching. This type of beading may be done in any of the formations just described—scattered, branched, or in lines. Several rows of beads can be laid next to each other to widen the line. Bugle beads are very effective in emphasizing the color patterns.

Beaded Edges

Decorative edges on vessels may add an element of surprise to an otherwise plain piece. The covering may be solid as with the covered-edges technique, textural with the branched-edge technique, or used to emphasize a color with the inside-outside technique.

COVERED EDGES

This is a loop of beads anchored on opposite sides of the edge, covering it completely. The number of beads strung will determine the depth of the loop on each side. Use an odd number of beads so there is a bead at the center of the turn and the turn does not occur between two beads. Anchor the thread, bring the needle to the right side at the desired distance in from the edge, and string on the number of beads necessary to cover the edge by the same amount on both the front and back sides. Pull the thread over the edge at a slight angle, and go through to the right side. Check that there is no bare thread; if there is, you'll need to either string more beads or shorten the distance between the anchor points. Make any necessary adjustments. Repeat in the same manner around the entire edge of the project, covering the edge completely.

BRANCHED EDGES

The branched technique (see "Branched Strands" on page 57) is also an effective edge technique. By starting some branches on the inside of the vessel and others on the outside, you can create a feathered effect on the edge (see the A J Hawks Vessel on page 49).

INSIDE-OUTSIDE BEADED EDGES

Beads that contrast with the rim of a vessel are stitched up to but not over the edge on the inside and outside of the rim. The thread edge of the vessel is visible between the beading, creating a beaded sandwich. The line technique (see "Beaded Lines" on page 59) works well for this edge finish.

THREAD SPRIG

The "sprig" for the Winged Squares Brooch is made from leftover thread.

A thread sprig is similar to a small tassel. It's created by wrapping thread around a square piece of cardboard to create a thread bundle. Once the bundle is formed, it's knotted at the center, folded in half, and secured at the knotted end. The thread at the opposite end can be left looped or trimmed even. Instructions for a basic thread sprig are given below.

1. Wrap thread 35 times around a 4" cardboard square (10 wraps each of silver and black and 15 wraps of red are shown here).

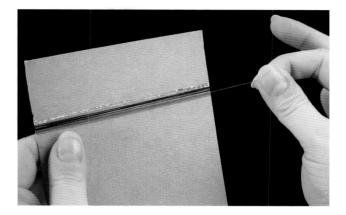

2. Slide the bundle of thread off the card, hold the ends, and tie an overhand knot.

3. To hold the uncut ends into a more upright position, wrap a 10" length of thread four or five times just above the knot, secure by tying a knot, and trim the thread tails.

Fringe

Decorative fringe may be added to a piece during the initial construction of the project, or you may add it later during the embellishing phase.

SOFT FRINGE

Make soft fringe by adding thread loops around the edge of a shaped and dry form, using four to six strands of thread in a hand-sewing needle. Anchor the thread on the edge and then form loops of the desired length, return to the edge, and anchor the loop with a whipstitch tight against the top edge before proceeding to make the next loop.

Soft fringe, added by hand with machine-embroidery thread, gives a wispy edge to a free-form bowl.

MACHINE FRINGE

Machine fringe is created by sewing a few stitches past the established edge of the form on the final round of stitching. The lines shouldn't be too close together, as that may create a soft, sloppy-looking edge rather than a well-defined, feathery fringe. It's a good idea to experiment on a scrap of stabilizer to determine the length and density of the stitching needed for the best effect.

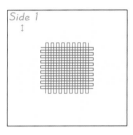

Either leave the fringe looped and uneven (see the All Blues Brooch on page 21), or cut it even when you trim the excess stabilizer from the work or after the piece dries. After dissolving the stabilizer but before the piece dries, shape the fringe in the desired direction.

Machine fringe adds a feathery appearance to the rim of a shallow vessel. Shape the fringe after dissolving the stabilizer in water. The dissolved stabilizer solution automatically stiffens the fringe, helping it retain its shape.

Resources

AllBrands
866-255-2726
www.allbrands.com
Needles, thread kits

AllStitch
410-646-0382
www.allstitch.net
Stabilizer, bulk machine needles

All Threads
877-237-5954
www.allthreads.com
Thread, stabilizer

Clotilde
800-772-2891
www.clotilde.com
Needles, thread

CreateForLess
866-333-4463
www.createforless.com
Stabilizer, metallic thread

Embroidery.com
800-428-7606
www.embroidery.com
Thread, stabilizer

Jane's Fiber and Beads
888-497-2665
www.janesfiberandbeads.com
Beads, beading supplies

Michaels
800-642-4235
www.michaels.com
Bead bars, findings, beads

Nancy's Notions
800-833-0690
www.nancysnotions.com
Machine needles, thread, darning foot

Rio Grande
800-545-6566
www.riogrande.com
Findings, pliers

Sew Fancy
800-739-3629
www.sewfancy.com
Free-motion foot, straw needles, machine needles, stabilizer by the yard

Sewing and Vac
800-544-5858
www.sewingandvac.com
Horizontal spool holder

The Sewphisticated Stitcher
866-210-0072
www.thesewphisticatedstitcher.com
Stabilizer by the yard, needles, thread

Sulky of America
800-874-4115
www.sulky.com
Thread, stabilizer

Superior Threads
800-499-1777
www.superiorthreads.com
Thread, needles, stabilizer, cone holder

ThreadArt.com
800-504-6867
www.threadart.com
Thread, spring tension hoops

About the Author

JANET HAWKS is a fiber artist who grew up in a family that created clothing and decorative items by knitting, crocheting, and sewing. Her exposure to and interest in fibers started early as she rode piggyback while her mother sewed on a treadle sewing machine. At age 6 Janet learned to knit, she was sewing all her own clothing by 15, and at 17 she learned to weave. These interests led her to a degree in occupational therapy from the University of Kansas and a career in rehabilitation medicine, which involved adapting craft activities to improve strength, coordination, and stamina in patients affected by neurological and muscular injuries.

Janet has also taught classes in Seminole patchwork and sewing with knits. She still does sew, weave, and quilt, but her current passion is sculpted threads. Visit her Web site at www.sculptedthreads.com.